MARIJUANA TODAY VANADIUM & URANIUM TOMORROW

MICKEY DEE

MARIJUANA TODAY VANADIUM &

URANIUM TOMORROW

Copyright 2019 by Mickey Dee

Frazier Publishing & Services

P.O. Box 363835

North Las Vegas, NV 89036

Table of Contents

INTRODUCTION

Marijuana and CBD's have taken the world by storm. They are in the process of interrupting whole industries like the medical industry. Companies are leveraging capital while making worldwide partnerships and expanding as they diversify. Several of these companies are emerging as leaders. We will take a look at the marijuana stock leaders a little later in the book but while marijuana is here today, let's take a look at vanadium and uranium for potential 100 baggers for tomorrow.

As the world moves away from fossil energies and non-renewable energy sources, the need for large-scale grid energy storage solutions continues to grow. Vanadium, in the form of Vanadium Redox Flow Batteries (VRFBs), has emerged as a likely solution due to their vast storage capacities, protection, and their ability to be charged and discharged tens of thousands of times without any loss in storage capacity. On the other hand, Uranium is the most widely used fuel by nuclear power plants for nuclear fission. The nuclear power plants, in turn, use the heat from nuclear fission to generate electricity. In the following chapters, I will discuss different aspects regarding uranium and vanadium as sources of energy.

CHAPTER 1

WHY URANIUM AS A SOURCE OF ENERGY?

Uranium is abundant, and technologies exist which can extend its use 60-fold if demand necessitates it. Global production is approximately 60, 000 tonnes annually, but a large portion of the market is being supplied from secondary sources such as supplies, including material from dismantled nuclear weapons. Below are the conversion levels of different sources of energy:

<u>Energy Conversion: Typical Heat Values of Various Fuels</u>

| Firewood (dry) | 16 MJ/kg |
| Brown coal (lignite) | 10 MJ/kg |

Black coal (low quality)	13-23 MJ/kg
Black coal (hard)	24-30 MJ/kg
Natural Gas	38 MJ/m^3
Crude Oil	45-46 MJ/kg
Uranium - in typical reactor	500,000 MJ/kg (of natural U)

MJ= Megajoules

From the table above, it is evident that uranium has the highest level of energy conversion. Therefore, uranium is the most efficient, cleanest and most effective form of energy because it has a longer lifetime compared to other non-renewable sources of energy. It is also reliable due to the relatively long-lasting supply of raw materials. Other than that, compared to other forms of energy, uranium does not emit greenhouse gases.

Is uranium poisonous?

Exposure to Uranium can lead to both chemical and radiological toxicity. Kidney toxicity happens to be the main effect connected with exposure to uranium. The toxicity can be caused by inhaling air containing uranium dust or by ingesting substances containing uranium, which then enters the bloodstream. Once in the bloodstream, the uranium compounds are filtered by the kidneys, where they can damage the kidney cells. High levels of uranium (50-150mg) can cause acute kidney failure and possible death. However, at lower levels (25-40mg), damage can be detected by the presence of protein and dead cells in urine. Additionally, at lower levels, the kidney repairs itself after several weeks after the uranium exposure has stopped.

Radioactivity of Uranium

Uranium is the heaviest atom present in the natural environment; however, its radioactivity is very low. It is a unique chemical element found in the earth's crust with an average of 3 grams per tonne. Additionally, its long life of several billion years has allowed the element to be still present. All isotopes of uranium are unstable and radioactive, though; uranium 238 and uranium 235 have half-lives which are adequately long to have permitted them to be still present. The half-life of uranium 238 is of 4.5 billion years whereas that of uranium 235 is only 700 million years.

CHAPTER TWO

HOW MUCH URANIUM AND VANADIUM DOES CHINA NEED?

Currently, China has the world's biggest nuclear building program. It has 37 reactors in operation and 20 of the 58 units presently under construction. Its annual uranium supplies are therefore now rising very fast, from 2,000 tonnes per annum in 2010 to around 7500 tonnes today and 11,000 tonnes in 2020. Trade statistics indicate that since 2010, China has imported 120,000 tonnes of natural uranium to add to domestic production of about 90,000 tonnes in this short period.

Vanadium, on the other hand, alleged to be the vitamin of metals has a wide range of uses in steel, chemicals, new materials, and energy. Before rising to the estimated 151, 000 tons in 2018, global vanadium production started to pick up in 2017 by 2.1% a year earlier to 148 tons of vanadium because the output in Brazil and China rose. As the world's largest vanadium producer, China reported a production of 48, 000 tons of vanadium (V205) in 2017, 3.3% more than the previous year, and a 57% share of the global total. With the increase in price and demand, China's vanadium output will keep increasing in the coming years at a reasonable pace due to the government's environmental campaigns and its prohibition on the import of vanadium. Presently, Vanadium Redox Batteries (VRBs) are responsible for less than 5% of vanadium demand. New vanadium demand is coming from China due to an increase in vanadium flow batteries used for large-scale energy storage. However, China has a plan to launch numerous pilot projects in the order of 100-MW-scale vanadium flow batteries by the end of 2020, therefore, if VRBs capture 25% of the forecast 10GWh annual market by 2025, energy storage will demand almost 14,000 tonnes of vanadium annually while each

GWh of VRB storage will require 5,500 tonnes of vanadium.

CHAPTER THREE

WILL THE JAPANESE DRIVE UP THE PRICE OF URANIUM?

The price of uranium is going to increase, and when it does, uranium explorers, producers, and stakeholders are going to get taken for an exciting ride. The uranium market is looking at a perfect storm of factors that are very good for uranium investors right now. Later we will look at companies that could possibly give you a return of over 1000% on your investment. In spite of its perceived risks, nuclear is a green form of energy generation that is emissions-free. The return to nuclear power for uranium-dependent Japan is taking place. As such, the global demand for U308 will likely increase because of the need for more power to run electric vehicles.

CHAPTER FOUR

WHERE DOES RUSSIA FIT IN?

Russia is moving steadily forward with plans for an expanded role of nuclear energy, including development of new reactor technology. Russia is committed to closing the fuel cycle, and sees fast reactors as a key to this. Also, exports of nuclear goods and services are a major Russian policy and economic goals. More than 20 nuclear power reactors are confirmed or scheduled for export construction. Russia is also the world leader in fast neuron reactor technology and is combining this through its breakthrough project.

Russia's nuclear plants, with 35 operating reactors totaling 26,983 MWe, comprise:

- 3 early VVER-440/230 or similar pressurized water reactors.

- 2 later VVER-440/213 pressurized water reactors.

- 12 current-generation VVER-1000 pressurized water reactors with a full containment structure, mostly V-320 types.

- One new-generation VVER-1200 reactor.

- 11 RBMK light water graphite reactors (LWGR) now unique to Russia. The four oldest of these were commissioned in the 1970s at Kursk and Leningrad and are of some concern to the Western world.

- 4 small graphite-moderated BWR reactors in eastern Siberia constructed in the 1970s for cogeneration (EGP-6 models on linked map) and due to be decommissioned by 2022.

- One BN-600 fast neutron reactor and one BN-800.

CHAPTER FIVE

WILL THE USA HAVE ENOUGH URANIUM? HOW WILL THEY GET IT?

The U.S gets its uranium from various countries as shown in the chart below:

Where U.S. Reactors Get Their Uranium
Purchases in pounds in 2017

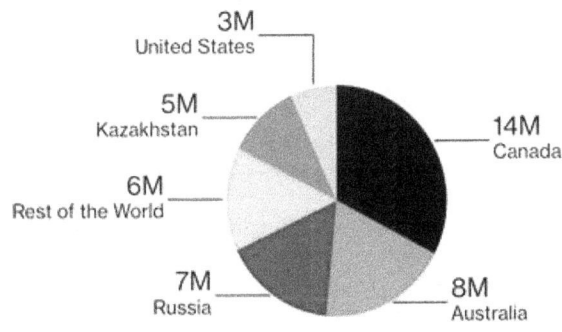

U.S. Energy Information Administration

The U.S.'s uranium purchases from Russia have entirely comprised of uranium recycled from Soviet warheads. However, relying on a Russian state-run nuclear company for U.S. nuclear fuel supply poses serious challenges in terms of the United States energy security. Additionally, the possible dangers of overreliance on foreign supplies in an increasingly competitive international market are highlighted by China's possession of the world supply of rare earth metals. Thus, given the growing demand for electricity and the number of new reactor builds planned, it is possible that the markets for uranium will only grow fiercer, placing the United States in a risky position if it does not develop domestic uranium deposits.

It's Not a Stretch to Conclude America May Have to Beg Russia & Canada for Uranium Just to Keep the Lights on

From the information above, it is evident that uranium and vanadium are the next big things in the energy industry. Russia is moving gradually forward with plans for an expanded role of nuclear energy, including development of new reactor technology. On the other hand, China has the world's biggest nuclear building program. It has 37 reactors in operation and 20 of the 58 units currently under construction. Also, with the increase in price and demand, China's vanadium output will keep increasing in the coming years at a moderate pace due to the government's environmental movements and its prohibition on the import of vanadium. Additionally, the potential risks of overreliance on foreign supplies in an increasingly competitive international market are highlighted by China's possession of the world supply of rare earth metals. Thus, given the increasing demand for electricity and the number of new reactor builds planned, it is likely that the markets for uranium will only grow fiercer, placing the United States in a dangerous position if it does not develop domestic uranium deposits.

Leading Marijuana Companies for Today

Name	Symbol	Exchange/Market Cap
Canopy Growth Corp	CGC	NYSE/11B
Aurora Cannabis Inc	ACB	NYSE/6B
The Alkaline Water Co.	WTER	NASDAQ/123M
New Age Beverage Corp.	NBEV	NASDAQ/433M
KushCo Holdings	KUSH	OTC/460M
Charlotte's Web	CWBHF	OTC/1.1B
Cronos Group	CRON	OTC/2B

Make Money Online with Cannabis Stocks, Learn This Basic Strategy and Build Wealth with Cannabis Stocks Today, by Mickey Dee, list over 40 cannabis stocks ready for major breakouts. In addition, Investing in Medical and Recreational Cannabis, Buy in Before, During and After Legalization, by Mickey Dee, is also available.

Leading Vanadium Stocks for Tomorrow

Name	Symbol	Exchange/Market Cap
Largo Resources	LGORF	OTC/1.2B
Westwater Resources	WWR	NASDAQ/11.3M
Anfield Energy	ANLDF	OTC/7M

Leading Vanadium and Uranium Combo Stocks

Name	Symbol	Exchange/Market Cap
Energy Fuels	UUUU	NYSE/318.3M
Western Uranium and Vanadium W	STRF	OTC/29.3M
Deep Yellow Limited	DYLLF	OTC/55M

Leading Uranium Stocks for Tomorrow

Name	Symbol	Exchange/Market Cap
Uranium Energy Corp	UEC	NYSE/225M
Ur Energy Inc	URG	NYSE/109M
Blue Sky Uranium Corp	BKUCF	OTC/14.2M
Cameco Corp	CCJ	NYSE/4.7B
Goviex Uranium	GVXXF	OTC/53M
Nexgen Energy	NXE	NYSE/677.7M
Azarga Uranium	AZZUF	OTC/34M
Millrock Resources	MLRKF	OTC/6.3M

The price of marijuana stocks will level off in the next couple of years and good earnings along with good management will dictate the price and direction of each company. If the price of vanadium and uranium continue to pull out of a multiple year bear market we could see all time blue sky breakouts in all of these stocks.

Bonus

Bonus Gold & Silver Stocks

Name	Symbol	Exchange/Market Cap
Kinross Gold	KGC	NYSE/4B
Barrick Gold	ABX	NYSE/15B
IAMGOLD	IAG	NYSE/2B
Eldorado Gold	EGO	NYSE/2.5B
Yamana Gold	AUY	NYSE/2.3B
Alexco Resources	AXU	NYSE/104M
Americas Silver	USAS	NYSE/74M
Wheaton Precious Metals	WPM	NYSE/8.6B
Equinox Gold	EQXFF	OTC/378M
Ely Gold Royalty	ELYGF	OTC/8M

Thank you for your support. Good luck with your investments and God Bless!